Winging It

WINGING IT

CHICKS WITH ZERO CLUCKS TO GIVE

SLOANE TANEN

Photographs by Stefan Hagen

BLOOMSBURY PUBLISHING
LONDON • OXFORD • NEW YORK • NEW DELHI • SYDNEY

BLOOMSBURY PUBLISHING
Bloomsbury Publishing Plc
50 Bedford Square, London, WC1B 3DP, UK

BLOOMSBURY, BLOOMSBURY PUBLISHING and the Diana logo are trademarks of Bloomsbury Publishing Plc

First published in 2003 as *Bitter With Baggage Seeks Same*
This edition published in 2019

Text © Sloane Tanen, 2003 and 2005
Photographs © Stefan Hagen, 2003 and 2005
This edition designed by Phillip Beresford (cover) and Charlotte Heal (interior)

Sloane Tanen and Stefan Hagen have asserted their right under the Copyright, Designs and Patents Act, 1988, to be identified as
Author and Photographer, respectively, of this work

For legal purposes the Acknowledgments on page 80 constitute an extension of this copyright page

A catalogue record for this book is available from the British Library

ISBN: HB: 978-1-4088-9939-7

2 4 6 8 10 9 7 5 3 1

Printed and bound in China by C&C Offset Printing Co., Ltd.

Bloomsbury Publishing Plc makes every effort to ensure that the papers used in the manufacture of our books are natural,
recyclable products made from wood grown in well-managed forests. Our manufacturing processes conform to the environmental
regulations of the country of origin

To find out more about our authors and books visit www.bloomsbury.com and sign up for our newsletters

FOR TRACY JAMES & AMY SCHEIBE

Maude was peeved. Her 3:30 yoga class was full again.
Didn't anybody work in this town?

Had Saffron fully grasped the excruciating pains of childbirth she would have insisted on the epidural from the first. Who cared what the doula would say? Next time, she might even plan a C-section, or just lay an egg like the rest of the girls.

Samantha looked around the playground in amazement.
Her mother had been right. She really was the smartest and the prettiest.

*A penny here, a penny there. One day Viveca would save enough
to have a Brazilian keratin treatment too.*

Cinderella didn't really mind being taunted by her stepmother and stepsisters.
She knew she was younger and hotter and that it was just a matter
of time until that divine prince from the party figured out her shoe size.
Besides, tales of her abusive childhood would be such a novelty at the castle.

Bridget had to ask herself if the "all over"
body wax had in fact been a very bad idea.

Helen knew all about the dangers of UV rays... but roasted,
baked or fried, she simply looked her best with a tan.

Dorothy couldn't believe she had to stand in line.
Didn't they know who she was?

Of course Mitchell encouraged Caesar's efforts to lose weight, but ever since he'd started the Atkins diet, Caesar's inexplicable mood swings and sweet meat breath had forged a wedge between them. As they lay in bed together not touching, Mitchell wondered if it was all worth it...

Marshall, Will, and Holly quickly realized there was
nothing routine about this expedition.

*Now well into their forties, the fellas sometimes wondered
if they should maybe start focusing on a different career.
Noooo way, dude... novooo way.*

Aviva had really enjoyed her upgrade to first class. Particularly delightful was the stewardess's smug swiping of the blue curtain that distinctly separated the preferred customers from the hoi polloi. But alas, as she was carted away with the other plebeians on the airport shuttle, it was the memory of those freshly baked chocolate chip cookies that illuminated her long-held conviction that she would indeed have to marry well.

Coco had explicitly said chocolate cake. Damn you Mother!!!

Yes, yes! Elvira did like piña coladas and taking walks in the rain.

*"I don't see a husband, children, or a career change in your future,
but I do see two adorable kittens."*

Paige didn't care. She knew she had right-of-way.

Mona had become increasingly irritated with Emily's
insistence that Saturday shopping always commence at Hermès.
After all, not all the girls had trust funds, and at 33, wasn't it time
Emily finally got a job? The girls often discussed what
Emily did all week anyway.

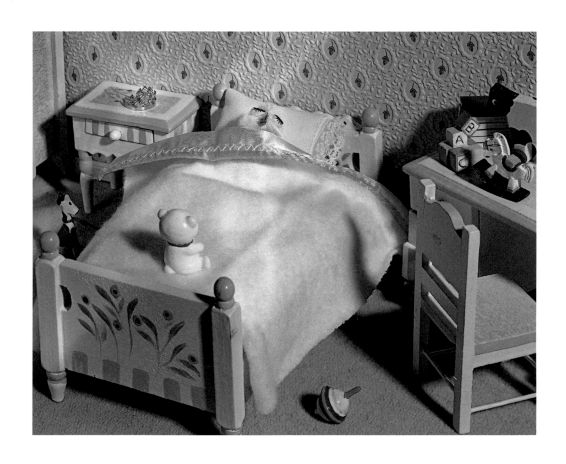

Coco dreamed that one day she would grow up to be
a benevolent queen... or a supermodel.

"But you ahh, Blanche, you ahh in that chair."

The Goldbergs really resented this holiday.

Anastasia was through making out with Ian.
He was never going to change.

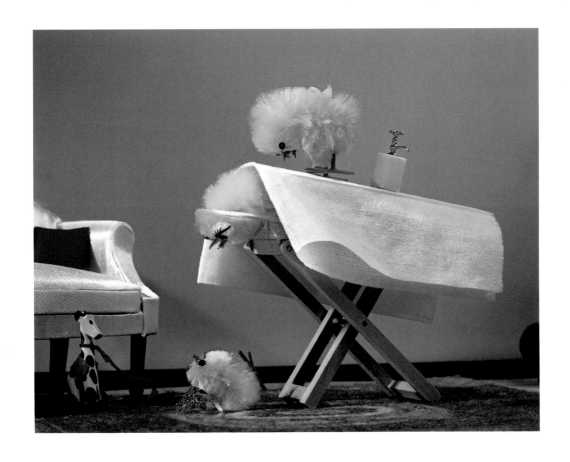

Coco felt that her mother's weekly massage was a fantastic opportunity to catch up on quality time.

Jay knew this script would sell. It was hot. Goodbye public transit, hello Ferrari. Goodbye wife and kids, HELLO Angelina Jolie.

"I don't know, the last thing he said was something about being king of the world, and then I may have accidentally pushed him."

An eerie silence quickly enveloped the Cohen family wagon. That last turn had been a grave mistake. They were no longer en route to California but heading south, deep into the heart of Kentucky.

#!@!!!

Ned was the only one who thought to look up...

On this, their fortieth-wedding-anniversary vacation, it looked as if both Mr. and Mrs. Prescott were finally going to get what they really wanted.

They called her fat, but Mama called her sturdy. They called her obstinate, but Mama called her ambitious. They said she wasn't graceful, but Mama said she was a powerhouse. And now the hefty little underdog from Keene Valley had won the gold. The only obstacle left was getting out of the arena without being tarred and feathered by Russia and Finland. Mama?

Mary Katherine blamed it on Mary Margaret and Mary Margaret said it was Mary Josephine. All Sister Agnes knew was that one of the girls was going down.

Abandoned once again in his padded bunker, Jonas plotted
a swift and sweet revenge. "Sleep with one eye open, Mother."

There was an old actress named Ruth
More than slightly obsessed with her youth
But no liposuction
Or deep reconstruction
Could soothe her like gin and vermouth

Now and again, Cinderella took a ride through the old neighborhood after a day of shopping. She felt it was important to keep in touch with the common folk.

Nipsey's bad manners left Coco speechless.

Boris the boy genius was stumped.

"*Back in my day we didn't ask which came first. There was a chicken, there was an egg, and that was good enough for us.*"

Caroline's eggs hadn't even hatched and already Victor's eyes were wandering.

Suzanne marveled at the fact that she was still single. Well, at least she had her vintage Judy Blume collection to keep her company on those long winter nights.

The ladies laughed and laughed and laughed. Now that would fix Rapunzel's wagon.

Coco was taken aback – she had never seen anything so lovely.

Desperado. He couldn't let somebody love him. Now it's too late.

Howie was stoked. He had finally penetrated the inner circle and soon he would be Dungeon Master. Then wouldn't everybody from school be sorry.

Minerva liked to stay indoors where the rooms smelled reassuringly of kasha.
The one time she had ventured out it was chilly and honestly quite frightening.

Paige was devastated to learn that Sarah Lawrence was not one of the Seven Sisters.
So what was the $250,000 for? Her first lesbian experience?

Goodnight Moon, hello martini.

The prince's perverse fantasies were beginning to take their toll on Cinderella.
Oh well, back to Barneys.

*Caitlin had memorized all her lines on the bus ride
in from Weehawken. She felt she was a shoo-in. But as she surveyed
her competition, her anxiety level reached a fever pitch. Not only
was she not the most beautiful girl in the room, she wasn't even pink.*

Carl wasn't exactly what Mindy was hoping for... but at least he was Jewish.

The tabloids reported that Cinderella had let herself go since the wedding.

"Ooooooooh!"

Weather, schmeather. It looked like a rowdy bunch and Bea wasn't getting on.

"You binge, I'll purge."

*Although Ed and Ted were born Siamese twins, regrettably,
their tastes in television programming had always differed.*

At $225 a session, Amy didn't want to talk about her intimacy issues.
She wanted to know what Dr. Arlow thought of her new shoes,
if he liked the bangs, and whether he too looked forward to their
weekly sessions with a gnawing anticipation.

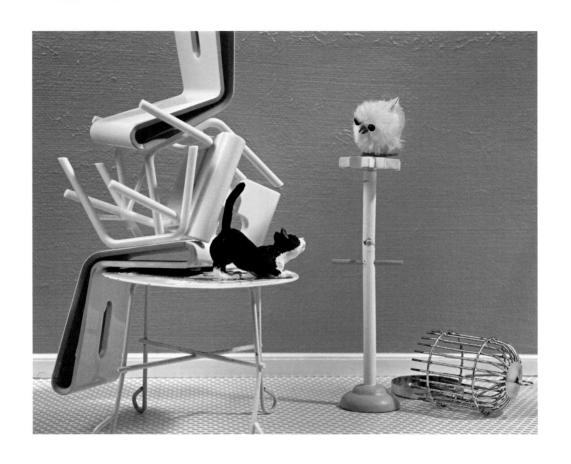

"For the love of God, man, stop calling me Tweety. The name's Nigel."

"Enough with the breadcrumbs already. Who's still eating carbs?"

"Oooohhh."

Reuben soon realized that the "family picnic" was just another of his parents'
schemes to trick him into exercising. As they finally neared the picnic table he felt he couldn't
be held responsible for what might happen if there wasn't a Twinkie in that basket.

ACKNOWLEDGMENTS

A very special thanks to Amy Williams and Colin Dickerman for making this project happen, and to Xa Shaw Stewart, Lea Beresford and Sarah Burnes for helping revive it. Deep thanks to Stefan Hagen, without whose beautiful photographs and tireless support, I'd have been lost. To Greg Villepique, Charlotte Heal, Phillip Beresford, Tree Abraham, and everyone at Bloomsbury for all their enthusiasm and hard work. Finally, I'd like to thank my family: Kitty and Larry for their endless support, Coco, Nick and Harry for their inspiration, my husband, Gary Taubes, whom I love more today than I did when the first chick hatched, and my father, Ned Tanen; I miss you every day.